Lest We Forget

Beyond The Battlefield

Edited By Donna Samworth

First published in Great Britain in 2024 by:

Young Writers
Remus House
Coltsfoot Drive
Peterborough
PE2 9BF
Telephone: 01733 890066
Website: www.youngwriters.co.uk

All Rights Reserved
Book Design by Ashley Janson
© Copyright Contributors 2023
Softback ISBN 978-1-83565-186-5

Printed and bound in the UK by BookPrintingUK
Website: www.bookprintinguk.com
YB0579U

Foreword

Our latest poetry competition, *Lest We Forget*, focuses on war and the impact it has had throughout the years. We asked young poets to pen their thoughts on the subject, either reflecting on the horrors of war, the impact on those left behind, or a hope for resolution. With conflict still rife in the world today, it's a subject that cannot and should not be avoided. It's important to acknowledge the sacrifices, fear and pain that some people still have to face, and these young poets have done just that.

Some of the poetry in this collection focuses on the direct experiences of war: the sights, sounds, smells and emotions, creating a vivid picture in the mind's eye. Other poets explore the difficulties faced by those who are left behind, and the emotions of waiting for your loved ones to return, uncertain if they ever will.

Here at Young Writers our aim is to encourage creativity in children and to inspire a love of the written word, so it's great to get such an amazing response. The result is a collection of thoughtful and moving poems in a variety of poetic styles that also showcase their creativity and writing ability. Seeing their work in print will encourage them to keep writing as they grow and become our poets of tomorrow.

I'd like to congratulate all the young poets in this anthology. However they chose to express their thoughts and feelings, the resounding effect is a powerful one: a continuous battle for freedom, hope, and above all, a cry for peace.

Contents

Hillsgrove Primary School, Welling

Mustafa Saeed (8)	1
Leyla Diabagate	2
Maysa Celik (8)	3
Hannah Heath (8)	4
Ella Crawford (8)	5
Elsie-Belle Maguire	6
Cordelia Surridge (9)	7
Rania Arif (8)	8
Noah Peters (8)	9
Charlie Brooks (8)	10
Eliza Miller (8)	11
Divyani Karki	12
Charlie Kirk (8)	13
Michael Jameson (8)	14
Joey Paddick (9)	15

International Community School London, Paddington

Michelle Evboifo (11)	16
Saana Seppala (14)	18

Joseph Norton SEMH Academy, Scissett

Shay Relph	20

Kirk Balk Academy, Hoyland

Patience Newman (13)	21
Maya Standrin (14)	22
Jake Wilde (11)	24
Emily Masterton (12)	25
Ebony-Mae Holmes (13)	26

Molly Whittham (12)	27

Kirkcaldy West Primary School, Kirkcaldy

Edith Lalande	28
Annabel Cuthbertson	30
Stefanija Saarna (11)	32
Murray Malcolm (11)	34
Scarlett Malcolm (11)	36
Maddison Reekie (11)	38
Charlotte Paddison	40
Max Malone (11)	41
Iona Morrice (11)	42
Valentina Franco (11)	44
Faith Williamson (11)	45
Abigail Anderson (11)	46
Mya Heriot (11)	48
James Duncan	49
Katie Sutherland (11)	50
Sadie Smart (11)	51
Kacie Ross (11)	52
Olly Marshall (11)	53
Filip Gorecki (11)	54
Violet Tasker	55
Luka Indopoulos (10)	56
Nikita Farmer	57
Lara Karambikova	58
Kacper Tomon (11)	59
Max McCulloch (11)	60
Cameron Hill (10)	61
Arabella Blacklaws	62
Tanuj Janarthanam Balamurali (10)	63
Kara Macdonald (10)	64
Oscar Tanco (11)	65

Lucy Sweaton (10)	66
Oliver	67
Stephen Chaplin	68
Taylor Swan (10)	69
Jack Fairfull	70
Jensen Galloway (11)	71
Martha Hobson (10)	72
Nairn Potter	73
Archie Learmonth	74
Angus Kennedy (11)	75
Anastassia Dorszewska	76
Cillian Williamson (11)	77
Emily Sweaton (10)	78
Poppy Ellis (11)	79
Rowan Murphy	80
Eden Mackie (10)	81
Carlisle Hutcheson	82
Harper Whyley	83
Mete Sener (11)	84
Coby Stewart	85
Raegan Russell (11)	86
Jonas Payne	87
Adam Percival (11)	88
Brandyn Robb	89
Julia Jakubowska (11)	90
Joao Romao	91
Adam Simpson (11)	92

Landau Forte Academy QEMS, Tamworth

Keeley Hilton (11)	93
Eleanor Price (15)	94
Ergean Ismail (11)	96
Emily Batten (14)	98
Caden Fallows (12)	100
Dylan Morton (11)	102
Olivia Harrison (14)	103
Thomas Langham (14)	104
Maria Sandu (15)	105
Beatrice Potirnichie (11)	106
Rosie Hadley (11)	107
Luca Bishop (11)	108
Maisie Jenkins (11)	109

Anton Alino (10)	110
Nedelina Stefanova (11)	111
Ashton Bulmer (11)	112
Katie Mason (11)	113
Aimee Jarratt (12)	114
Terlea Tune (11)	115
Eliza Price (11)	116
George Stokes (12)	117
Isabelle Caile (15)	118
Tommy Rooke (11)	119
Tristan Boyce (11)	120
Olivia Lawson (12)	121
Bethany Hunt (11)	122
Mia Plant (14)	123
Samuel Martin (11)	124
Samuel Rochfort (11)	125
Mitchell Flounders (12)	126
Reece Evans (14)	127
Xenon Dunn (14)	128

Leeds East Academy, Seacroft

Harriet Broughton-Read	129

Lings Primary School, Lings

Alanna Collis (4)	130

Loughborough Amherst School, Loughborough

Phoebe Jakubas (13)	131

Louth Academy, Louth

Tobias Wiltshire	133

Marshgate Primary School, Richmond

Charlie Sheldrick (9)	134
Aahil Upil	135
Lily Schofield (10)	136
Clara Anstey	137
Vienna-Pervin Upil (9)	138

Ivor Richmond (9)	139
Cormac Lavery (10)	140
Rohan Dinan (9)	141
Dogu Goktepe (9)	142
Molly Conneely (9)	143
Isla Vannet	144

Medina College, Newport

Jenson Byrne (11)	145
Lucy Archer (13)	146
Georgia Wilkins (11)	147
Leland Arnell (13)	148
William Barbero (12)	149
Jack Day (11)	150
Bubbles Barton (11)	151
Chloe Lewin (12)	152
Jessie Goring (11)	153
Nicholas Waghorn (13)	154

Nicholas Chamberlaine School, Bedworth

Bryony Roberts	155

Northview House School, Kilbarchan

Brooke Till	156

Norton Canes High School, Cannock

Summer Morris (14)	158
Lacey-Mae Owens	159

Oldbury Wells School, Oldbury Wells

Apryl Jennings (12)	160
Ben Morris Baker (11)	161

Parklands Academy, Chorley

Jenny Queally (12)	162
Izzy Frohock (12)	164
Safiya Zentani (15)	166
Hind Fares (13)	168
Róisín Cunningham	169
Raghad Elhabal (14)	170
Lincoln Stothers (15)	171

Portsmouth High School, Southsea

India Akass (11)	172
Iris Hu (11)	174
Alice Hu (11)	175

Queenswood School, Hatfield

Mia Rosenberg (14)	176
Issy Naylor (15)	177

The Poems

The Soldier

I know what the life-sacrificing soldier feels, alas!
When the sun peeps round the curtains
When the taste of freedom approaches him but it slips right out;
Love of a family comes to him but the noise goes and it's all forgotten;
When the hugs of a family wraps him like a blanket;
When the first drop falls and the first cloud arrives;
When the first child raises and the last one hugs
I know what the life-sacrificing soldier feels!

I know what the life-sacrificing soldier sticks his hand to the gun
Until his life flies the skies of nothingness
It causes hallucinations and pain
He must kill the enemies, if not it will cost him his life
He feels annoyed and disappointed
I know the soldier sticks his hand to the gun!

I know what the life-sacrificing soldier dreams
Giant scares reminding him of sadness
The peace of a life and joy of a time
It isn't a dream of love
Yet it is a dream of death and explosion
Till he goes up to the skies above
I know what the life-sacrificing soldier dreams.

Mustafa Saeed (8)
Hillsgrove Primary School, Welling

Sacrifice On The Field

I know what the powerless soldier feels, alas!
When the taste of freedom disappears into thin air,
When the comfort of a loving family slowly slips away
And the calm, cosy beds drifting away like sand
When the first poppy blooms and the first sun rises
And the relaxing warmth of food grows in his tummy -
I know how the powerless soldier feels!

I know why the powerless soldier kills his mortal enemy
Till they give up in despair
For he must win the mighty battle for his country
When he escapes his bloodthirsty nightmare
And recurring sleepless nightmares
And his heartless, isolated heart is full of despair
I know why the powerless soldier kills his mortal enemy!

I know why the powerless soldier hugs
With his bloody open wounds hurting from head to toe
When his open freedom is snatched away along with peace and harmony
It is not a positive hug of glee
But a deadly hug of despair
But to the stars above his head -
I know why the powerless soldier hugs!

Leyla Diabagate
Hillsgrove Primary School, Welling

The Fierce Soldier

I know how the fierce soldier feels, alas!
When he brings back memories of his cosy comfortable home;
When he had forgotten the feel of his soft clothes
And the calming peace like the waves of the ocean,
When the first poppy grows and the first wind blows,
And the taste of the peaceful freedom - I know how the fierce soldier feels

I know why he fights the enemy
Till it starts to get hot and sweaty
For he must protect his country
He must end the bloodthirsty war to protect himself from death
He causes endless tears and heartbreak,
He is still scared of his humiliating nightmares,
I know why he fights his enemy!

I know what the fierce soldier dreams of,
Sadly they lost all hope and some of his friends got seriously injured,
He really wants to end the war and be free,
This is definitely not a dream of love,
Instead it's a humiliating, bloody nightmare
All he wants is to go back to his peaceful, cosy house
I know what the peaceful soldier dreams of!

Maysa Celik (8)
Hillsgrove Primary School, Welling

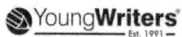

The Soldier's Life

I know what the tired soldier feels, alas!
When he remembers the love of his family.
When his taste of love gets lost
And his memories of clean soft clothes like a warming hug disappears
When the first rain falls and the first bird sings
And the fresh smell of flowers he once smelt has gone
I know how the tired soldier feels!

I know why the tired soldier can't sleep at night
Till he is set free
He doesn't know when his enemies will come
He must protect himself so he does not die or get killed
Pain and nightmares enter his brain.
He feels frightened and devastated
I know why the soldier can't sleep at night.

I know why the soldier longs for a hug
When his open wounds and scratches come
And he is wishing to end this horrible war.
When he wants a hug
It is not a warm, happy hug of love
It is a hug to save himself from getting killed
He wants to go to Heaven and above the clouds
I know why the soldier longs for a hug!

Hannah Heath (8)
Hillsgrove Primary School, Welling

The Powerless Soldier

I know what the powerless soldier feels, alas!
When the feeling of love is coming any day
When freedom will never come back again
And he dreams of clean, cosy, hot clothes like a blanket
When the first child laughs and the first rain falls
And the taste of a warming hug of joy lingers
I know what the brave soldier feels!

I know why the shooting and firing every day comes and goes
Till his fingers are bursting with pain
For they can beat them and never come back again
When he defends his country it's still here
Escape this nightmare, never come back
And it causes hallucinations and ends lives
And he is heartbroken and sad.

I know why hugs are loved and warming
When his wounds are open and lives are calling -
When freedom is never coming back again
It is not a hug or a warm touch
But it is peace and love
But it is not a nightmare, it is the stars above
I know why hugs are loved and warming!

Ella Crawford (8)
Hillsgrove Primary School, Welling

The War-Torn Soldier

I know what the powerless soldier feels, alas!
When the quiet, calming peace is around the curtain
When the taste of freedom stirs through the air
And the comfort of family is always there
When the first child laughs
And the first sun rises
When he feels clean, cosy clothes for the first time
I know how the soldier feels!

I know why he keeps his gun close, alas!
Till he has bruises and scars like how stars disappear
For shooting and killing is getting out of hand
When he knows he must win for his family
And end this bloodthirsty war
And the pain still comes from his old scars
I know why he keeps his gun close!

I know why he hugs himself
When he goes to bed scared from head to toe
When he wants to return home and see friends and family
It's not a time for joy or glee
It is a dream for love and freedom
It's a bloody nightmare to the stars above
I know why he hugs himself!

Elsie-Belle Maguire
Hillsgrove Primary School, Welling

The First War

I know what the powerless soldier feels, alas!
When the taste of freedom wafts through the air
When he has forgotten the comfort of clean clothes
And wishes he could hold his cute, cuddly pets like a warming hug
When the first ocean waves and the first poppy grows
And the nice peace and quiet makes a hush in the world
I know how the powerless soldier feels!

I know why the powerless soldier crawls across the floor
Till he can't go any further
For he pleads to escape this hell
He plans to end this bloodthirsty war!
Hallucinations start to take over his mind
And he is down in the dumps with nothing to do
I know why the soldier crawls across the floor!

I know why the soldier dreams
When his sight is lost and he cannot breathe -
When he stops the war and he can go home
It is not a dream of happiness
But a bloody nightmare of death
A void of darkness
I know why the soldier dreams!

Cordelia Surridge (9)
Hillsgrove Primary School, Welling

War Sympathy

I know what the war-torn soldier feels, alas!
When he remembers the comfort of loving family,
When the taste of freedom slowly slips away,
And the cosiness of clean clothes fades away like a feather in the wind
When the first poppy opens and the first wind blows,
When the sun's beating ray gets stolen -
I know what the war-torn soldier feels!

I know why the soldier kills his enemy
He will fight until he is free;
For he must be ready to defend when he ends this bloodthirsty war;
And the bloody heart with the recurring nightmares
And the isolated, down-in-the-dumps soldier bleeds -
I know why the soldier kills his enemy!

I know why the soldier dreams
When the poisoned gas goes in his deep wounds -
When he faces freedom and wins for his country,
It is not a song of peace and harmony,
A hug of death squeezes tight
But he hopes to go to the stars above -
I know why the soldier dreams.

Rania Arif (8)
Hillsgrove Primary School, Welling

The Powerless Soldier

I know what the powerless soldier feels, alas!
When he misses the taste of freedom that flies through the air,
When the air springs through the grass,
And the memories of clean clothes fade away like a feather or some leaves.
When the first child laughs and the poppy opens,
And the peace and harmony of the world is shattered.
I know what the powerless soldier feels.

I know what the powerless soldier feels
When he holds his gun tight
When there is nothing left
When the enemy does not like the gun on him
When he wants to stay alive
When he feels sick and mad
I know what the powerless soldier feels

I know why the soldier sings, oh my
When he is dying from gas
When he wishes for the war to end
When he sings and dreams
In the fight to the death
In the war there is the everlasting star
I know what the powerless soldier sings.

Noah Peters (8)
Hillsgrove Primary School, Welling

The Injured Soldier

I know what the injured soldier feels, alas!
When he misses the taste of freedom;
When the comfort of family slowly slips away,
And the memory of clothes fade away like sand,
When the first ocean waves and the first poppy opens,
And the silent, calming peace is shattered -
I know what the injured soldier feels!

I know why the injured soldier kills his enemy
He must hold his gun because he does not know when his enemy will come
He must win this battle and this bloodthirsty war -
I know why the injured soldier kills his enemy!
I know why the injured soldier dreams
Again and again, he gets open bloody wounds
All he wants is freedom and to go home,
He dreams of death and horror,
One night, he sent a plea to the stars up above -
I know why the injured soldier dreams!

Charlie Brooks (8)
Hillsgrove Primary School, Welling

The First Poppy

I know what the tired soldier feels, alas!
When his pets hug him and love him
When the clean, cosy clothes love him
And good food feels like a waving family hug
When the first poppy opens and the ocean waves
And the clean bed with love and care
I know what the tired soldier feels, alas!

I know why he can't sleep
Till the bomb has gone
For the people that die and cry
When he must end this bloodthirsty war
And he is feeling lonely, hopeless and sad
I know why he can't sleep!

I know why a tired soldier feels sad!
When the infected, scarred, bloody wounds grow
When he wants to go home
It is not a hug of harmony
It is a hug of death
But I want to go to Heaven -
I know why a tired soldier feels sad!

Eliza Miller (8)
Hillsgrove Primary School, Welling

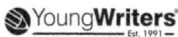

The First War

I know what the war-torn soldier feels
When the taste of freedom slowly slips away.
When the comfort of a loving family is all he wants,
When he misses his clean, comfy clothes.
When the first sun rises and the first baby can be free.
He kills his enemies during battle.
He is free once they are gone.
He must be ready to defend his land.
All he wants is to protect his wonderful family and friends.
He feels the pain throb in his heart.
He is so upset and down in the dumps.
He dreams of being free and out of the trenches.
With missing limbs and horrible scars.
His freedom is all he wants.
He desperately misses love and warmth.
Death is lying in a pool and being dejected,
He wants peace and to live in heaven.

Divyani Karki
Hillsgrove Primary School, Welling

War Soldier

I know what the war-torn soldier feels, alas!
When the taste of freedom sweeps through the air,
When he pulls his cosy and comfy cover over his head,
Wishing to see his cute, cuddly pets like the coat of love,
When the sound of ocean waters and the first buds opens,
And the world saying a plea and harmony making it feel like paradise -
I know what the soldier feels!

I know how he holds his gun tight,
For he must fight a bloodthirsty battle,
He must be ready to sacrifice himself for the Great War -
When his empty heart pounds and it goes all heavy!

I know why the heart pounds as it goes all heavy.
I know why the soldier timbers a log to the stars
When the canopy of worth turns into a hug of death!

Charlie Kirk (8)
Hillsgrove Primary School, Welling

The Soldier

I know what the heartbroken soldier feels alas!
When the memories of family creeps into his head,
When the soldier needs the love of his wife,
When he misses the laughter of his friends,
When he misses the loving hugs of family and friends,
When the first poppy grows and when the sun rises,
And the peace and harmony of the world is shattered -
I know what the heartbroken soldier feels.

I know how the sad soldier feels,
He's getting his guns ready to shoot;
Till they start fighting back,
For he must fight till the end,
He feels sick and ill and pain rocks his body,
The soldier feels like he's at the bottom of a pit -
I know how the sad soldier feels!

Michael Jameson (8)
Hillsgrove Primary School, Welling

The Soldier

I know what the soldier feels, alas,
He kills his enemies until he can't shoot any more,
Stitches all over his body, pain in his heart;
Wanting to escape the army and return to his family and friends who he misses with all his heart,
No escape till he ends the war,
His dreams of humming and singing and a life of love,
He hates the killing and longs for a life to go home -
He prays to heaven it will end.
I know what the soldier feels.

Joey Paddick (9)
Hillsgrove Primary School, Welling

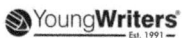

In War And Peace

Battles waged, our world ablaze,
Soldiers marching, in a daze,
Weapons clash, the cries they rise,
In this war, no one survives.

But amidst the chaos, let us pray,
For a tranquil world, where peace holds sway,
Where brotherhood and love unite,
And darkness fades into the light.

Let's lay down arms and heed the call,
To mend the wounds, to stand tall,
To find solace amidst the strife,
And build a future, free from knife.

War ravages, leaving scars so deep,
Destroying lives, making hearts weep,
But we must find the strength within,
To embrace peace, let healing begin.

For peace is not a distant dream,
It's a reality, or so it seems,
In our hearts, it starts to bloom,
A sanctuary where hatred finds no room.

So let us strive to end this war,
To mend what's broken, to restore,

A world where love outweighs the fight,
And peace prevails, with all its might.

In war and peace, we have a choice,
To listen to our heart's own voice,
And stand together, hand in hand,
For war to cease, in every land.

Michelle Evboifo (11)
International Community School London, Paddington

Long Distance

Every time I see him my problems go away
No one else can make me feel this way
I feel happiness
I feel joy
I feel safe
When I'm with him,

Yet he has to go away
We're both sad
Even though we're together
We're both scared
Even though we're together
Because we won't know when we'll see each other,

Instead of feeling happy
We feel there's a time limit
Until one of us has to go
Too many things to do
Not enough time
We don't know where to go
Or what to do

I don't know when he will come back
So I can feel safe again
In his arms
I can only feel safe

Feel peace
Once again

He's the only one who understands me
No one else knows me
Unlike him
He understands what I feel
Even without the proper words
We are like two love birds
Lost in the woods
Finding a place to nest
So we can finally be together
And rest.

Saana Seppala (14)
International Community School London, Paddington

The War

The war was bloody
Many men died through the war
It was atrocious

Soldiers charged
The sound of gunfire filled the air
Booming black smoke covered the battlefield

A mess of bodies
Littering the muddy ground
Tanks rolled past, rolled past, rolled past.

Shay Relph
Joseph Norton SEMH Academy, Scissett

Goodbye

They say their last goodbyes
And off he goes,
Shuddering breaths
Fears of what's coming,
Left, right, left, right
Down the fields into the trenches,
The first shot and it starts.

Suddenly the air fills with cries of battle,
Bang!
One drops...
Bang! Bang!
Two more honoured bodies collapse.

Only three days of battle before it all ends,
Bang!
He was hit,
The world blurred as tears dripped down his face,
Red flows from his chest,
And he falls.

Today his daughter walks along the church,
Poppy seeds scattered on the ground,
And she looks up at the name engraved on the stone slab,
Tears fall.

Lest we forget!

Patience Newman (13)
Kirk Balk Academy, Hoyland

Poppies

Lest we forget,
The sacrifices they made,
Lest we forget,
Their courage unswayed,
Lest we forget,
The suffering and cold feet,
Lest we forget,
The soon-to-be widows shifting in their seats
Lest we forget,
The many lives lost,
Lest we forget,
The lines that they crossed,
Lest we forget,
The ones that were shot,
Lest we forget,
And so we do not.
Lest we forget.

We lay down the poppies,
As a sign of respect,
We lay down the poppies,
And reflect.
Every year on the eleventh minute,
Of the eleventh hour,
Of the eleventh day,
And in November at the graves,

We stay.
Lest we forget.

Maya Standrin (14)
Kirk Balk Academy, Hoyland

The Poppy Of Death...

The great war, that started it all,
Bombed fields, dead bodies
One poppy

Started 1914,
The Commander passed already,
His remnants, left on the battlefield,
One poppy, it spread its seeds,

The smoke-filled air,
Lift the seeds afloat,
Taking them across the red fields of blood

They settle at the dead soldiers,
Sprouting into a full-grown poppy,
That one poppy, that started the spread,
It spread like wildfire.

That symbol of death and peace,
The war,
Lest we forget.

Jake Wilde (11)
Kirk Balk Academy, Hoyland

Remember, Remember

Remember, remember the 11th of November.
It's an important day that everyone should remember.
The men that fought for their country,
All the families that fled their homes.
We need to appreciate this gesture.
All the casualties and battles
Just over a small, little argument.
Wear a poppy to show your love
For the amazing soldiers who sacrificed their lives.

Lest we forget.

Emily Masterton (12)
Kirk Balk Academy, Hoyland

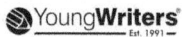

When The War Is Over

Bullets soar screeching in the air,
Men lay low in the trenches,
Fallen men flood the ground, leaving echoing anguish,
Deafening bombs explode, the sound lingering in the air,
Birds fill the sky, softly dropping letters from loved ones,
Silence fills the eerie, dark sky.
Is the war over?

Ebony-Mae Holmes (13)
Kirk Balk Academy, Hoyland

Little Poppy

Little poppy as small as can be,
Sitting in my pocket, eating my tea,
On my desk when I lay,
Helping guide me on my way.

Little poppy as small as can be,
You mean everything to me,
Reminding me of the stars in the sky,

Little poppy you keep my eyes dry.

Molly Whittham (12)
Kirk Balk Academy, Hoyland

The Bun

I really wanted food,
But Mother was in a mood,
So, I went to the bakery the shopkeeper was rude,
If only I could have a little food.

I needed food before the bombs dropped fast,
I needed food before the guns were cast,
I needed food or I would not last,
I could not put this in my past.

I moaned,
I groaned,
I went to my friend's he loaned me a pence,
I climbed over the fence.

I passed the shop window,
It had luscious buns,
I really wanted one,
But the shop was closed the day was done.

As I went home the Wardens fled,
Making me puzzled in my head,
The air sirens blasted red,
If I died where would I go instead?

The next day I wanted to steal,
One of those buns it would make a good meal,
I stared into its golden glory,

Lest We Forget - Beyond The Battlefield

It was enough to appeal,
The shopkeeper made a deal,
Only if I didn't steal.

I was in a dream,
As I took a heavenly bite,
It was enough to please me the little mite.

I went right home,
I didn't moan or groan,
In that unruly tone,
That was louder than the phone.

As I walk in,
My face had a grin,
So shiny and gleaming like a metal tin,
It would never go to the bin.

As I went to bed,
A voice inside my head,
Led me to the goodness of being fed,
And my stomach was a little more rounded.

I remembered my father away at war,
No longer knocking at our door,
Walking along our wooden floor,
And now I think I need him more.

Edith Lalande
Kirkcaldy West Primary School, Kirkcaldy

We Fight

We fight for our town, we fight for our country,
Fight for the timeline, fight for history,
Fighting every minute, fighting every day,
Fighting for each of the homes we stay,

Listened to his rules, listened to his plot,
Agreed with everything that he thought,
But then he went too far, then he wouldn't stop,
So instead, we agreed and fought,

The bombs dropped fast day and night,
Killing many people, what a sight,
Soldiers in the air, soldiers on the ground,
Fire in the air, and massive sound,

We fight for our town, we fight for our country,
Fight for the timeline, fight for history,
Fighting every minute, fighting every day,
Fighting for each of the homes we stay,

People in their homes, maybe they're alone,
Waiting for the ring, ring, ring of the phone,
Wanting the good news, that they need to hear,
Otherwise, there could be some tears,

We won't be destroyed, we won't be defeated,
Just got the urge that we needed,

Lest We Forget - Beyond The Battlefield

We will go to victory party and parade,
How about a glass of lemonade?

We fight for our town, we fight for our country,
Fight for the timeline, fight for history,
Fighting every minute, fighting every day,
Fighting for each of the homes we stay,

Now we must remember, about this special time,
All about when Germany committed a crime,
Remember the soldiers, remember the crew,
And remember to pass this down from you.

Annabel Cuthbertson
Kirkcaldy West Primary School, Kirkcaldy

The Evacuation Time Poem

Evacuation started, everyone panicked,
I looked outside but kids were crying,
my mum came in and told me to pack,
I was confused but my mouth was shut,
The next thing I knew my mum was packing,
I asked her what was wrong but she said nothing.

Later on, I got my information,
my mum said out loud evacuation,
I was shocked but had to take it although I wasn't happy,
I looked down straight on the floor feeling sadder than ever,
with my new news, I went and had a bite to eat,
but then I had to stop, I went and sat at the window,
but minutes later my parents joined,
when they hugged it was the best feeling but sadly it was my best and last.

I heard a noise so I peeked outside,
but all I saw was a train waiting,
I took my bag and with tears in my eyes,
I hugged my parents and said goodbye,
I started walking and got inside sitting in a seat,
Around me were sad-looking kids that made me want to cry.

Later on, I heard bombing so I closed my ears and shut my eyes,
hours later I opened my eyes realising I was sleeping,

I looked outside and said I was here,
I came out arriving at the countryside seeing my new unfamiliar parents.

Stefanija Saarna (11)
Kirkcaldy West Primary School, Kirkcaldy

Heart Of The Soldier

Some of the soldiers are not alive,
But they expect us to thrive.
Even where the cattle sleep,
You can hear the gunshots deep and deep.
As the soldiers fight from dawn to night,
If they are witnessed they are shot on sight.

Back at home the bombs drop,
At the time Nazi Germany was on top.
As the battle goes on and increases,
Our next generation are left to pick up the pieces.
These soldiers fighting still have love,
But when shot they fly up like a dove.

At the battle, when it rains,
Most soldiers pass away in pain.
The soldiers are away from home,
So, they have the right to moan.
As the dead are put in their grave,
They were the heart of the soldier.

As the Nazi's planes fly overhead,
The soldiers shot lie in the medical bed.
Our supplies were missing but they don't care,
As their roar, was like a bear.
As the soldier's mothers, tears run from their eyes,
After all, it is the second war in this franchise.

When the soldiers fade out in the cities,
They were the heart of the soldier.

Murray Malcolm (11)
Kirkcaldy West Primary School, Kirkcaldy

The Light That Doesn't Shine At Night

In the sky, it is black at night,
The lack of light gives me such a fright,
I have to carry my mask as an ordered task,
I would definitely rather pass before the gas,
My father is away at war for so long,
there is no one to sing me my bedtime song.

When there's silence there will be no violence,
There are no sirens to dictate the estate on how to keep us safe,
The Germans couldn't be anything else but burdens!
No one is brave enough to stand up to Hitler's rage.

All I see are posters every time I go out after dawn,
I shut the door peacefully before I give a big yawn,
To save a life don't show a light, just try to fight for our rights,
When it's black at night we must attack,
I never leave the house at night so I really don't get a fright,
and all I want to see at the parks are the bright yellow kites.

When I'm dreaming all I see is guns,
I hear them I must run, they must be near,
Run, run, run!
I hear roars of bombs in the sky. "Hitler can you stop!" I swore.

My mother says everything will be fine,
but we all know that's a little white lie.

Scarlett Malcolm (11)
Kirkcaldy West Primary School, Kirkcaldy

What Happened During The Blitz?

The Blitz began, the sun set low
And no one knew they'd meet their foe
Soaring through the sky, the German soldiers travelled by
Dropping bombs on every house
The noise sounded louder than a mouse
The piercing sirens went through my ears
Making everyone end up in tears
Bomb after bomb
Plane after plane
The sky was set with a blood-red flame
Britain was destroyed
The planes fell from above
Lots of people had died, even a dove
The buildings were destroyed, they caught fire
The flames became higher and higher
The ground was dry and the sky was lit
The air smelled like a bottomless pit

Everything was loud, you could even hear guns
But the German soldiers weren't done
They would keep on bombing, went on for hours
Everyone was in their Anderson shelters

I'll never forget September of 1945 when I felt loads of glory
After a while they finally left and that's what happened
during the Blitz.

Maddison Reekie (11)
Kirkcaldy West Primary School, Kirkcaldy

Children Of 1945

We, the children of 1945
Lay on the ground, wishing to be alive
We cry on the ground, thinking in vain
For those who don't care about our suffer and pain

As I fall into the depths of sorrow
I long for a life, that I could borrow,
But of course, I am here very lonely
Because what they did was really unholy

Germans drop bombs on us, thinking it's a game
Hoping to kill us and drive us insane
But my biggest thing of a desire
Is to set the Nazi's house on fire!

Oh, how far we could go if it wasn't for them
Oh what I would give for strawberries and Kreme
The dreams I dreamt nearly came true
But it all went wrong after the crossed the line we drew

So now I descend from the world I once knew
I will never forget the land and the bottomless blue
I will never stop seeking for the future I still want,
But be careful Germans, because I will haunt.

Charlotte Paddison
Kirkcaldy West Primary School, Kirkcaldy

The Last Day

Through the damp, through snow, freezing cold,
Minute by minute soldiers died,
Seeing people, saying goodbye,
And people not even saying bye,
Hearing people bawl and cry in the far far distance
Every night, lights are out not a peek of light or you won't see day again.

Do what you're told, even if you're old,
Kids crying, parents dying,
Putting on your mask, air getting thin,
Bombing in the city, people getting gritty,
Every family in a pity
Planes up and down, bang bang on the ground.

People having no homes because of bombs,
Hitler's plan coming, not going to plan,
Shoot them down, wait, are they one of theirs or is it one of us?
People in a different house, with people with a strange house,
Not like my house, not like anything where my mum and dad loved.

Max Malone (11)
Kirkcaldy West Primary School, Kirkcaldy

A Day In The Life Of A Soldier

A soldier's day is never done,
Always up for your bread
Looking out for the sun at dawn.
Wishing that you could have stayed in bed
Whilst the sun shone,
It is always everyone for their own.

See to the guns a many
Briefing at six, must be early
Off into the sky
Barely still alive
Nearly about to die

Everyone has to get it right
The formation has to look neat
Trying with all our might
To stay in our seat
This fight is dangerous
But death is more
Especially in the dead of night when no one is sure.

We all have one vision
To save the nation
To make a decision
To get all the formations

And not a collision
But most of all to have the sensation
And to start the celebration
For the war is done and we have won.

Iona Morrice (11)
Kirkcaldy West Primary School, Kirkcaldy

The Banging Of The Bombing

The bombing that I hear is banging in my ears,
the things that I see from my point of view,
might be why I am so blue,
I always hear the bangs and don't know what to do,
unless I see him in my view,
It's always so scary which makes me weary,
I can't stop crying I might be dying.

I'm always running to my assigned tasks,
with my heavy gas mask,
I'm constantly hearing the bombing of the banging,
which isn't calming,
Bang! Bang! Bang! There goes the banging,
someone's probably hanging.

I can smell the gas I can see the task,
I'm always hearing the bombing wanting to go home,
but I'm always staying here in this zone,
During daylight moonlight still it goes,
The banging of the bombing always flows,
Everyone telling me it will be alright,
but we all know that's just a lie.

Valentina Franco (11)
Kirkcaldy West Primary School, Kirkcaldy

Bitter, Damp Shelter

While bombs are dropping all around,
The deceased are resting without a sound,
As bullets fly, as bullets pelter,
I am safe in my bitter, damp shelter.

In this dump of a hole,
Made of corrugated iron,
My house is burning,
My house is on fire,
I have one thought, one desire,
That I could set their fury on fire.

For causing us so much pain,
The German Nazis are whom to blame,
It is dark and mucky and so moist too,
If I did not think of it as muck,
I would think of it as poo,
The roof is damp and covered in moss,
But all those soldiers have been lost,
Because bullets fly, bullets pelter,
But I am safe in my bitter, damp shelter.

Although it's damp, although it's mucky,
I suppose I am pretty lucky,
Because soldiers are dead, they are peltered,
As they do not have a bitter, damp shelter.

Faith Williamson (11)
Kirkcaldy West Primary School, Kirkcaldy

Air Raid

Once the sirens go,
It is very scary,
So, don't be contrary,
Be very weary.
I know it's not fun,
but you just need to run.

The bombs drop very fast,
and make a huge blast,
but don't worry,
it will eventually pass.

I understand it's tiring,
when the bombs are firing,
but if you get shot by a gun,
you are definitely done,
and that wouldn't be fun.

The shelters are a dread,
well at least you're not dead,
you can get really bored,
but when you get out it feels like a reward.

The Germans always linger,
and drop bombs at the click of a finger.
Just try not to worry because the soldiers,

will eventually become closer,
to making sure that Hitler won't take over.

Abigail Anderson (11)
Kirkcaldy West Primary School, Kirkcaldy

Bombing Blackout

Soldier's day just begun,
No birds were singing except one,
The sky was red and everyone was in their bed,
No one to be seen because all of them were dead.

No lights, no fires, no nothing,
Only seeing black for me,
In the plane I go,
Wondering when I can go home,
No time to choose when the truth must die,
No time to lose or say goodbye.

I need to run because they have a gun,
I only see one of my sons,
One by one till the day is done,
To my grave I go with a crow on my stone,
With scattered bones around the poppies that will always grow,
We will always remember 1945 when lots of people died,
They didn't even have time to say goodbye,
But families will fly and will look up in the sky.

Mya Heriot (11)
Kirkcaldy West Primary School, Kirkcaldy

Air-Raid Poem

Suddenly air raids, planes shoot in the sky,
And pilots hoping that they don't die.
As their loved ones cry and some of them saying goodbye,
Some can wake up but not say goodnight,
Some saying goodbye even when it is daylight.

Most of them bombing cities and families are in pity
All the grounds are getting gritty
The first day they leave families asking them to stay.
While Hitler is killing all the gays

Every day families pray some more
Kids want to play but they all have to move away
Hitler killing the Jews
And families are not able to choose about who they lose.
A lot of people smelling gas as the Germans break all of the glass,
Of the shops and so do the cops.

James Duncan
Kirkcaldy West Primary School, Kirkcaldy

Up And Down

As the guns fire,
The gas leaks from the sky,
The bell rings and wakes us from our tire,
My oh my in the sky,

Sigh of relief
From my grief

Clamp went the guard's boot on the wet floor,
I woke up startled as the guard stopped at my door,
I got my breakfast it had been one year,
Since the white flag went up and everything got dear,

He gave people jobs, he got them power,
He killed his opponents, or he put them away,
From their homes where they could not stay,
He made the people cower, from his power,

One night he disappeared,
With a bang, a smash and a thud,
No longer to be seen again,
Thank goodness he was such a pain.

Katie Sutherland (11)
Kirkcaldy West Primary School, Kirkcaldy

The Reign Of Terror

As the bombs keep dropping
People's hearts keep stopping
Down in the streets below
It fills me up with sorrow
People lying dead in the street
With death they will meet
Bullets and bombs are raining down
On our little town
People screaming and running around
An awful deathly screaming sound
Kids and parents crying for the ones they love
They're looking up at them from above
Buildings and houses come falling down
Spreading fire along the ground
The Anderson shelters are all destroyed
Falling bombs, we need to avoid
Now it is quiet, not a sound can you hear
Now all the people who passed have no fear
The Nazis have gone, they refused to stay
And now the Nazis will have to pay.

Sadie Smart (11)
Kirkcaldy West Primary School, Kirkcaldy

Soldiers' Demise

Violently pulling on our gas masks
Filling up the air we well know this could be our last task
The red sky is awfully silent
Then it's ferociously violent.

As the ash-black night sky sets
We throw our war-worn guns to rest
As we launch up in the sky
We can feel our family's cry, they do not want us to die

When we hear the roaring fire of guns
We know the clock strikes time to run
And grab our blood-ridden guns as the grey sky looms
Above the moon we all experience the feeling of mass gloom

I just want more nutritious food
But the cold-hearted commandant shook
One shake of his scarred head, the merciless German wants us dead
And my legs feel as stiff as lead.

Kacie Ross (11)
Kirkcaldy West Primary School, Kirkcaldy

During The War

Staring at the pitch-black sky,
Listening as the bombers fly,
The Nazis have not set foot in Britain,
But still the damage has been hitting.

Missiles dropping left and right,
Soldiers preparing for a fight,
Even if they don't come home,
They'll be grateful they won't rest alone.

Air-raid wardens in a line,
Even a cigarette could get you a fine,
Deafening sirens bursting my ears,
Though I'm grateful that they're here.

Praying the bombers can't see any light,
'Cause then our future won't be bright,
Black material on our doors,
That all happened during the war.

Olly Marshall (11)
Kirkcaldy West Primary School, Kirkcaldy

The Day To Remember

Poppies, oh poppies, the remembrance flower.
It's for the brave
Who fought with great power
As the lower class died, food was the only thing they craved.

During the great world war, it was tremendous,
The poppies grew and grew as people fell dead.
Many deaths and injuries made this battle horrendous
Many families fled.

As soldiers walk through Flanders fields,
They see bloody red poppies.
The guns of murder that they yield,
Are responsible for all the corpses and bodies.

Today we remember
The day the Nazis surrendered.

Filip Gorecki (11)
Kirkcaldy West Primary School, Kirkcaldy

Best Friends Forever!

Bang!
Ears ringing
Thousands of gunshots in the distance,
As loud as a thunderstorm!
"Not much longer my friend!" he shouts over the crashing bombs
"We can do it!"
Screams piercing his ears,
Getting tired with the weight of his friend
"I can't go on!" wails his friend
They collapse to the ground
"I'm holding you back"
"Go on without me"
Slowly he walks away
Tears pouring down his face
Sadness taking over him
Leaving his friend to die,
To die alone...

Violet Tasker
Kirkcaldy West Primary School, Kirkcaldy

Welcome To World War I

In Flanders fields the poppies blow,
There is where we eat and sleep and drink,
The planes in the sky cross and row,
We're all on the boat hard thinking.

In the sky, that is where it marks our place,
Between France and Germany the guns blow,
We never get what we want in the war we praise,
Germany thinks with food they can glow.

Marching in the cold day,
The bombs flying in the sky,
Wanting to go and play,
Now everyone has nearly died.

Marching home now, we're happy,
We're nearly all home.

Luka Indopoulos (10)
Kirkcaldy West Primary School, Kirkcaldy

WWII

Welcome to WWII.
Look out, here it may be treacherous.
We may have a lot to do.
And here in WWII it is very dangerous.

Here in WWII we fight for family.
And we live in the trenches.
Beware because the bombs come suddenly.
In memory of loved ones we build benches.

People get bombed at every hour.
And when the siren goes it tells all of us to take cover.
They normally go for the big towers.
And we normally lose contact with our brothers.

The poppy is the flower that reminds us of the soldiers.
And beware of the falling boulders.

Nikita Farmer
Kirkcaldy West Primary School, Kirkcaldy

Remembrance Day Poem

Our soldiers work for us, never forget to remember.
Silence performing from the sky.
The month we remember is called November.
And they were never ready to say goodbye.

The wars ended and everything went silent.
Poppies shining as red as the blood.
So much war, depression and violence.
They probably had a blood flood.

Watching memories tear apart with a shiny poppy.
I hope you angels fly.
And I hope you watched us copy.
Tearful eyes that made us cry.

Rest in peace, I hope you remember
We will never forget November.

Lara Karambikova
Kirkcaldy West Primary School, Kirkcaldy

WWII Poem

WWII is a big scene
And it is very intense
There have been absurd things we have seen
So, we give out all of our defence

The Nazis have attacked our home
And have destroyed many buildings
Through our streets they were able to roam
So the soldiers tried to stop the killings

Evacuees got taken to the countryside
And got put in host families
They got taken on a big ride
And the people got in big insanities

WWII was a big journey
And you can tell me if it was worthy.

Kacper Tomon (11)
Kirkcaldy West Primary School, Kirkcaldy

The Sadness

Boom!
Bombs going off from every corner of the pitch-black sky
A mysterious soldier dashing to his wounded friend
Blood gushing out of his friend on the verge of death
Sadness creeping through his soul
Bang! Bang!
Gunshots from the darkened forest
He sprinted into a murky, smelly hole
He felt like he'd been shot 1,000 times.
The raging gunfire finally stopped after hours
The soldier came out of the hole
The man rushed back to camp
Safe
By a miracle from God.

Max McCulloch (11)
Kirkcaldy West Primary School, Kirkcaldy

WWII Sonnet

An evacuee is what I am
And I am 10-year-old
My mum said to stay calm
And that was what I was told

Our soldiers fight for our country
But fighting is quite scary
And there are bombs dropping monthly
And things are getting worse already

But the atomic bomb was invented by the Americans
And drops them on Japan
Which leads to another of our wins
And everything has gone according to plan

Almost everything is back to normal
But the past is still very dull.

Cameron Hill (10)
Kirkcaldy West Primary School, Kirkcaldy

WWII Poem

This is WWII
Where kids are being evacuated to the countryside
Where there's nothing to do
But their carers are full of pride

They're scared because they're away from home
Where they can't sleep at night
And they feel very alone
And their family have to fight

They're still not totally safe
But safer than in the city
They're being very brave
WWII is such a pity

They will hopefully be home soon
At night they stare at the moon.

Arabella Blacklaws
Kirkcaldy West Primary School, Kirkcaldy

World War I

World War I, the deadliest war in history
Everywhere bombs are exploding
Soldiers need a lot of bravery
Letters they are forbidding

There is no time for peacefulness
Hear the explosions and jump up and down
There is only time for deadliness
There is no time for a clown

Soldiers we remember for bringing us peace
Poppies we keep for remembrance
There is no police
There is so much violence

Everywhere there are boulders
Thank you to the soldiers.

Tanuj Janarthanam Balamurali (10)
Kirkcaldy West Primary School, Kirkcaldy

WWII

Here you are in WWII
Hitler is a dangerous man
All of what you heard is true
Even the things about Anne

Anne Frank had a very special diary
We were on limits for food
Why do we always have anxiety?
The war is not that good

I feel sorry for the people Hitler killed
Propaganda is always on the streets
We always had to drink milk
Some people are not that sweet

We build benches to remember our men
And hope we never go to war again.

Kara Macdonald (10)
Kirkcaldy West Primary School, Kirkcaldy

Spanish Civil War

Smoke, piling up like rubble and debris.
The smell of smoke and gunpowder blocks my scent.
I can hear screams of agony in the distance.
Bang!
The sound shatters my ears.
I fall to the ground, my ears ringing so loud I can only hear my own breath.
The rifle now feels ice cold in my hands.
Determined, I get up and keep moving.
"Vamos, vamos! Nos van a matar!" screams my friend.
A storm of debris is charging towards me.
I'm knocked out cold...

Oscar Tanco (11)
Kirkcaldy West Primary School, Kirkcaldy

World War II

Welcome to World War II
Where little kids in the countryside are scared
They don't know what to do
Them and strangers get paired

Men have to go to war far, far away
It must be sad for the evacuees
There is still war to this day
All the children should be free

Sadly, some cry at night
Although it is unsafe
Soldiers have to fight
So, they are staying brave

There are so many dead trees
The soldiers' souls should be free.

Lucy Sweaton (10)
Kirkcaldy West Primary School, Kirkcaldy

World War II

Welcome to World War II
A place of hate and horrid
We have a lot to fix
So, let's hope we're supported

Me and my friends live in the trenches
And my family hope they don't get bombed
We also have to sleep on dirty benches
So, we just have to be calmed

The Nazis have no heart
And we have no food
So, we just have to be smart
And no one should be rude

The war is coming to an end
So now we can all be friends.

Oliver
Kirkcaldy West Primary School, Kirkcaldy

WWII Poem

We are in WWII.
All we do is fight for our team.
We have a lot to do.
We hope this is just a dream.

We have a lot of air-raid shelters.
For when we get bombed.
We have a lot of helpers.
And everyone needs to be calmed.

We are constantly rationing.
Every last bit of our food.
People don't have a lot of fashion.
And some people are so rude.

We have a lot of power
And the poppy is the peace flower.

Stephen Chaplin
Kirkcaldy West Primary School, Kirkcaldy

WWI

Welcome to WWI
It is a time in history
Sometimes people had guns
And then the allies finally got victory

Over 40 million got killed
The poppy is a remembrance flower
A lot of the holes were filled
People got shot every hour

It was scary at first
But after the war it got better
Some people died of thirst
There were loads of sweaters

People had a lot of power
And the poppy is a peace flower.

Taylor Swan (10)
Kirkcaldy West Primary School, Kirkcaldy

WWII

This is WWII
Here danger is everywhere
We all have a job to do
Nothing will come, not even a bear

Our families are in the countryside
For it is the only safe place
For all we know they could've died
I keep guns in a safe case

Me and my friends are in trenches
Every hour people die
And in memory we build benches
I always let out a huge sigh

When people get shot
They bleed a lot.

Jack Fairfull
Kirkcaldy West Primary School, Kirkcaldy

Is This War?

Is this war or is it life?
It feels more like both,
But with much more strife
And my only comfort is to loathe

All this death is very sad.
I do not know why this even happened,
And I see it all as very bad.
I am starting to feel very maddened

I don't seem to understand why people have war
It's pointless and bad
But people just do it more
Or is it just because they are mad?

People who make war are bad
And I call that sad.

Jensen Galloway (11)
Kirkcaldy West Primary School, Kirkcaldy

Remembrance Day

Together we will work
We will go out to war
The other soldiers lurk
What are we fighting for?

We do two minutes of silence
To remember the people who died
There was lots of violence
Lots of people cried

Poppies are our flower
They help us remember our men
They fought with great power
So they could come home again

We have benches to remember
And Remembrance Day is in November.

Martha Hobson (10)
Kirkcaldy West Primary School, Kirkcaldy

Friendship

Why did you have to leave me here all alone by myself?
Why couldn't you last another week, why?
Tears streaming down my face
I feel so guilty
I should have been there
I could have saved you
Standing here makes me feel sad
I'm heartbroken
Bang!
Gunshots firing
Birds tweeting
Branches cracking
I'm sorry
Rest in peace
You have found your final resting place
Goodbye!

Nairn Potter
Kirkcaldy West Primary School, Kirkcaldy

The Reign Of The Young Man And His Plane

A young man found a plane,
That had a gun that started his reign,
Little did he know that plane,
Would end in pain.

Lots of soldiers running away,
But the man and his plane took their lives away,
Bombs dropping on the field below,
The man couldn't help but chuckle at the death and sorrow.

But now the young man was old,
But still flying his plane he encountered another young man,
In his plane that took his plane and life away.

Archie Learmonth
Kirkcaldy West Primary School, Kirkcaldy

Longing To Get Home

Looking at the horizon
Smoke coming from ships
Planes flying above the water and the beach
Gunshots firing
Piercing through my ears as loud as a whip
Ships being loaded
I need to get down there
Poppies are growing behind me, it is so beautiful
My gun and helmet are getting colder
Bombs still dropping, hopefully I don't get hit
It's busy now
Soldiers wanting to get home!

Angus Kennedy (11)
Kirkcaldy West Primary School, Kirkcaldy

Crazy War

This is WWII
It's very scary here
I don't know what to do
My dad drinks lots of beer

I always try to escape
The bombs won't stop
Everything is a mistake
Everyone around me just drops

I try to run to the trains
It's literally hard to escape
Every time it just rains
My family always relates

I have to go to the host family
How does everyone live there so happily...?

Anastassia Dorszewska
Kirkcaldy West Primary School, Kirkcaldy

Defeat

I can smell the sickening scent of blood,
Gunshots ringing in my ears,
Enemies getting closer!
Last goodbyes,
Friends dropping like flies,
Gunshots shattering their bodies,
Shattering my heart.
Blood trickling down my face,
They're even closer now,
Closer than ever,
It's over,
We've lost,
Goodbye,
Bang!

Cillian Williamson (11)
Kirkcaldy West Primary School, Kirkcaldy

War

People get hurt
Everybody fights
Because their house gets burnt
But they end up with no light

We try to stop the war
All we get is trench foot
But it all goes too far
Even though we wear boots

We all want our families
We have no food
We want it to go happily
All we do is work for wood

We want to finish this war
What are we all fighting for?

Emily Sweaton (10)
Kirkcaldy West Primary School, Kirkcaldy

The Lost Soldier

Oh, my friend, why did you leave me here all alone?
I am ashamed I didn't save you in time
I've fallen into a spiral of guilt thinking about you
Why was it you and not me?
Bombs and guns screaming in the distance
When will it all end?
I am heartbroken without you my friend
I need you!
Rest in peace until we meet again!

Poppy Ellis (11)
Kirkcaldy West Primary School, Kirkcaldy

Last Love

Why oh why?
You could have lived!
Bombs blasting in my ear!
I'm super guilty.
Blood dripping off my head
Gas spreading everywhere!
People shouting on the horizon
Planes dropping bombs
He was an angel in my heart
Bombs screaming in my ears
I'm petrified!
Goodbye my dear friend.

Rowan Murphy
Kirkcaldy West Primary School, Kirkcaldy

Lost

Why did you have to die?
What do I do without you?
I'm lost
Alone
Cold tears running down my face
I'm sore, hungry and lost
The smell of smoke and blood is making me feel sick
Only one more week till this war ends
I'm lost
I should have been there
See you soon my brother.

Eden Mackie (10)
Kirkcaldy West Primary School, Kirkcaldy

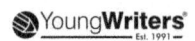

War Poem

I hope for a better future.
We wear poppies.
There is a very bad culture.
There is always a gun copy.
The USSR is very powerful.
Not just at war.
And not so peaceful.
Most of us have swore.
Hopefully peace can unite.
We don't cry.
Although we fight.
Because we try.
It's never quiet.
And it's always a riot.

Carlisle Hutcheson
Kirkcaldy West Primary School, Kirkcaldy

Best Friends Forever

Running as fast as he can
Weight of his friend slowing him down
Blood crawling down his dirty face
He carefully sat his friend down
Bang! A gunshot
His friend slowly dying
Sad he couldn't save his friend
He had to leave him
As he left he said 'best friends forever'.

Harper Whyley
Kirkcaldy West Primary School, Kirkcaldy

Lost Soul

Why couldn't you have lived another week?
Without you I am nothing
I miss you
If I had been there next to you
I could have saved you
Now I am standing next to you alone
Why did you need to die?
I wish you were here next to me
See you on the other side
Rest in peace, my friend.

Mete Sener (11)
Kirkcaldy West Primary School, Kirkcaldy

The Letter Home

Bombs banging around him,
He started to write his letter home,
The wind blowing his pages,
People screaming in the distance,
Gunshots flying through the bright blue sky,
The bomb exploded right next to him,
Bang!
Blood running down his cheek
He slowly died!

Coby Stewart
Kirkcaldy West Primary School, Kirkcaldy

Wait, Aim And Shoot!

Smell of gunpowder making me nervous
Trees rattling in the wind
Bang!
A loud bomb goes off
Aiming my gun at the soldier in front of me
Sneakily hiding behind protection, ready to shoot
Bang!
One soldier down
Nineteen more and one tank to go.

Raegan Russell (11)
Kirkcaldy West Primary School, Kirkcaldy

Phantom Friend

Hello!
It's almost over
Shells and bombs exploding
It's not fair
I'm the one who should have died
Cries of pain in the distance
My brother fallen like an angel
It's never going to be the same
To fall just before freedom
Goodbye, brother.

Jonas Payne
Kirkcaldy West Primary School, Kirkcaldy

Battle Of Okinawa

Fire burning in the soldier's ear
Leaves twirling like a hurricane
Gunshots are as fast as a bomber plane
Guns reloading in a second
Planes crashing in the background
Soldiers slowly dying
Waves crashing on the shore
Last time going into the forest...

Adam Percival (11)
Kirkcaldy West Primary School, Kirkcaldy

The Poppies Flow

As the poppies flow soldiers suffer from the terrible war
As you try to ignore the roar from the war
The poppies are red like the blood of the dead
The parents are sad, houses destroyed
Children left homeless when darkness subsides
Bombs and guns, stray dogs run.

Brandyn Robb
Kirkcaldy West Primary School, Kirkcaldy

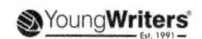

The Happy Ending

Oh when will the war end?
Bullets crashing through the sky.
My gun is as cold as ice
You can smell the smoke coming from the red and deep fire.
People dying
Confidently aiming
Bang!
The man falls to the floor.
Shaking I drop the gun.
Finally the war has ended!

Julia Jakubowska (11)
Kirkcaldy West Primary School, Kirkcaldy

War Poem

I lay in bed,
The sky turned red,
I ran outside,
Many died,
I tried to run,
I had no one,
Then I stopped trying,
I started crying,
I lay there praying
Then I started dying.

Joao Romao
Kirkcaldy West Primary School, Kirkcaldy

Sad

Soldier slowly dying
His cold fingers touching his face
Mud all around
Crying everywhere
Gunshots bang!
Soldier down.

Adam Simpson (11)
Kirkcaldy West Primary School, Kirkcaldy

Lest We Forget

War starts with an argument from both sides.
A disagreement that can't be resolved.
Tanks and bombs strike fear upon the land.
And screaming scared children gripping tightly their mother's hand.

The courage of soldiers fear for their lives.
Their families sit quietly crying silently inside.
Not knowing when they'll see their loved ones again.
The feeling of terror and trauma adding to their pain.

Homes with blackout curtains to hide the light.
Not knowing when the sirens will go off.
Ordinary people living in extraordinary times.
Death and destruction rain down from our skies.

People walking through the streets buildings flattened.
The smell of burning fabric and rubble scattered everywhere.
Feelings of anger and fighting talk inside.
And wondering when it's all going to end.

Our freedom is important to us all.
Hoping for peace and tranquillity in our lives.
Forever to be thankful to the fallen.
And lest we forget.

Keeley Hilton (11)
Landau Forte Academy QEMS, Tamworth

Love Has Broken

I do not want war,
I do not want my world to turn to dust and ashes,
by the anger of some men,
in a country many of us have never set foot in,
please,
come home,

I do not want my young, free head,
to be filled with blood and tears,
images no one should have engraved in their mind,
I do not want to be left with jagged edges of so many broken dreams,
of every friend, neighbour, every life ever worth living,
now endevoured too deep into this emotional whirlwind of destruction,
please,
come home,

I know nothing of hate,
for I am just a child,
yet I am afraid if it continues to grow,
bigger bigger bigger bigger bigger,
until one day it can not grow anymore and we are left.
Everything reduced to ghosts and shadows,
please,
come home,

I beg and I beg,
what a good person they are,
who deserves not to become a ghost nor shadow,
but to live and laugh,
cherish our family,
watch me grow,
please,
come home,

This war has ended all hope,
love has broken,
life is lost,

yet everybody talking calls this a solution,
no other way,
no better way,
is what they all call,
war,
is no solution,
but despair for every soul unlucky enough to be alive,
because death road to hell,
would be more finer than this,

Goodbye Dad.

Eleanor Price (15)
Landau Forte Academy QEMS, Tamworth

The Horrors Of War

In the darkest hours, where shadows creep,
A world consumed by conflict, war so deep.
The sadness engulfs, a heavy weight to bear,
As lives are shattered, beyond repair.

In the trenches, where soldiers stand,
Their courage unwavering, a united band.
With hearts of steel, they march on,
Fighting for freedom, until the dawn.
But amidst the chaos, a glimmer of light,
The hope for peace, shining so bright.

In the hearts of children, so pure and true,
Lies the power to change, to start anew.
For innocence lost, in the horrors of war,
Must be met with compassion, for evermore.

In their eyes, we see a future so bright,
Where love and understanding can make things right.
From different perspectives, we must learn,
To break the cycle, and let peace return.

For in understanding, we find our way,
To a world where conflicts no longer sway.
And in the silence, on Remembrance Day,
We honor the fallen, as we kneel and pray.

Their sacrifice, a reminder profound,
That peace is a treasure, to always be found.

Ergean Ismail (11)
Landau Forte Academy QEMS, Tamworth

Remember

The innocent children lying in bed,
Who don't know if their fathers are alive or dead,
Wounds so bad the leg may be amputated,
Gunshots and explosions ringing in the air,
Many soldiers shot down dead,
Their uniforms turning red.

The sirens ringing down their ears,
The sound of the last day for some,
Thousands never breathed again,
While the fortunate got home to tell their story,
The disease-ridden trenches that they called home,
Caused many to die from infections and gangrene,
Whilst others died of starvation and exhaustion.

For those with mental health issues,
Many were shot for cowardice,
Very few were sent home,
They needed numbers on the front line.

On the 11th of November every year,
People from all over the world gather,
To pay their respects to the fallen,
At 11 o'clock there is a two-minute silence,
Across the world, everybody is silent,
'Lest we forget' is read in many services,

Flags drop and hats removed
And last post is played on the bugle.

Emily Batten (14)
Landau Forte Academy QEMS, Tamworth

The Struggles Of War

First thing in the morning, we see the dawn,
Staring back at us as we yawn,
At last, the sun rises,
Making us hope for new surprises.

Making our way to our guns,
We cannot visit our loved ones,
On the move, all the time,
Leaving our shelter, out we climb.

Marching forward, there is no going back,
For as the other side might attack,
Never give up, never back down,
Is our motto when we are out of town.

Finally, as we catch a sight,
We hope to make this over with tonight,
Firing first, we have the advantage,
Making sure we can manage.

Hoping we were far from this place,
Memorising our loved ones' embrace,
Crawling our way through mud,
Trying not to swallow innocent blood.

Two years later, I am a survivor,
My sister was happy to see me back, it's like I revived her,

My family were in tears too,
They said there is a whole new future because of you.

Rest in peace to all that died during war.
Lest we forget.

Caden Fallows (12)
Landau Forte Academy QEMS, Tamworth

What Is Going On In The World Today?

What is going on in the world today?
The fighting and killing must stop without delay.
It's on the news every single night, in Israel, Ukraine and Palestine.
The skies light up with a crash and a boom, while the rest of the world looks on with gloom.

The streets and the cities are quiet like a church mouse, no cars, no people, no children out laughing and playing.
The only noises are the siren warning, the zooming of war planes overhead and the dropping of bombs.
All you can hear is the shouts and the screams and little children crying for their moms.

The destruction and devastation is clear in the morning - Homes, schools and shops all flattened just like the tide coming in at night over a sandcastle built on the beach.
So I ask myself is peace really that far out of reach?

Why as a world can't we all just get along and replace hate with love and war with peace
And maybe we can create a world to be proud of and a real masterpiece.

Dylan Morton (11)
Landau Forte Academy QEMS, Tamworth

Lest We Forget - Beyond The Battlefield

Thank You, My Friend

As I lie here in pain,
I can feel the fear running through my veins.
I remember that fateful day.
When I was full of dismay.
I'm scared, I'm hurt,
And I'm lying here in the dirt.
Bombs falling all around.
Bullets scattered on the ground.
I wish this day wasn't true.
But, it was for me and you.
Your courage for me John,
When all of my hope had gone.
Your bravery saw me through,
And now I have a chance to say.
Thank you.
As my grandchildren hold my hand,
And I prepare to enter your land.
As I reflect on all of my years,
I am thankful for all of those happy tears.
The family that I have made,
The memories that begin to fade,
Have all been possible because of you.
My comrade, my saviour, my friend.
They say Lest We Forget,
But there is not one moment I regret.

Olivia Harrison (14)
Landau Forte Academy QEMS, Tamworth

Never Forget

We make a serious commitment in the dimness of time to remember those who gave their lives in order to save us. Lest we forget, there are still heroes out there whose bravery and valour are evident.

Their souls persist and their lessons are delivered in distant places where battles were waged.
Day and night, brave troops marched to protect the cause of freedom with bright hearts.

Their memories cherished in every silent prayer, their names inscribed in history, eternally preserved.
We work towards a world where peace replaces their selfless acts of grace, lest we forget.

From the depths of the trenches to the sky above, their sacrifice demonstrates an unending love.
Fears aside, their honour unwavering and never amiss, they approached the unknown.

They exist, gone but not forgotten.

Thomas Langham (14)
Landau Forte Academy QEMS, Tamworth

The Peace We Hope For

In trenches deep, where horrors dwell,
Men march to where the dark clouds swell.
War's cruel song, a haunting knell,
Echoes loud, a tragic spell.

Fields once lush, now scarred and bare,
Whispers lost upon the air.
Minds burdened, burdened hearts despair,
As battle's fury lingers there.

Families torn, their hopes entwined,
By conflict's grasp, so unkind.
Sorrow's shadow veils the mind,
In war, no peace, no solace find.

Yet in this chaos, a fervent plea,
For peace to reign, for all to see.
To heal the wounds, to set minds free,
And end the cycle of enmity.

Let swords be sheathed, let voices soar,
To find resolve and strife ignore.
For in unity, a world restore,
Where love and kindness will outpour.

Maria Sandu (15)
Landau Forte Academy QEMS, Tamworth

Echoes Of Battle

In times of conflict, battles waged with might,
Where darkness falls, and hope takes flight.
Soldiers brave, their courage shining bright,
In the theatre of war, where day turns to night

Machines of destruction, the thunderous roar,
Leaving scars on the land for evermore.
Families torn, hearts heavy with pain,
As war's cruel hand leaves its lasting stain.

But let us dream of a world at peace,
Where hatred and violence forever cease.
For in unity and love, we shall find our way,
To a brighter tomorrow, a more hopeful day.

In the midst of chaos, may hope arise,
And in every heart, let compassion be the prize.
For the scars of war can heal with time,
As humanity strives for a world sublime.

Beatrice Potirnichie (11)
Landau Forte Academy QEMS, Tamworth

Lest We Forget

L iving surrounded by war is tough
E veryone off fighting, trying to make it stop
S adness overtaking the citizens of all countries
T he bombs going bang, crash, pop.

W e will always remember these historic events
E ach one of us won't forget.

F or the soldiers who sacrificed their lives for us, we give thanks
O thers surviving but never the same again
R est in peace to the innocent people lost
G rief consuming those left behind, left them feeling pain
E veryone hoping for peace one day
T hese are the wars, the soldiers, the sacrifices we will never forget.

Rosie Hadley (11)
Landau Forte Academy QEMS, Tamworth

11/11...

My great-grandad served in the war
Because the other country broke the law
A hero I never got to meet
But 11/11 is where we remember all

I'm proud to see my uncle serve in the RAF
The sacrifice he makes is to keep us safe
He inspires me to be great
But 11/11 he'll be my mate

The sadness of the war in Ukraine
Where innocent people are in pain
The children must be so scared
But 11/11 showed that we cared

These events have inspired me to join the army
Because I want to be able to protect my country
And help my fellow friends aim for one thing
Because 11/11 is where we all hope for peace.

Luca Bishop (11)
Landau Forte Academy QEMS, Tamworth

To Be Unforgotten

Behind a poppy is more than just a seed,
it's a person just like you and me.
A person who's risked themselves,
for a better life for someone else.
They fought and battled for life to be good,
and so for that we remember as we should.
They didn't have to try for a better outcome,
those times of pain were the last for some.
And soon the time comes to cherish,
all those people to sadly perish.
For some what they gave up was a high price,
their lives were huge to sacrifice.
And so here I am writing this poem,
so we all remember.
To show our appreciation,
within our nation.

Maisie Jenkins (11)
Landau Forte Academy QEMS, Tamworth

Lest We Forget

We will never forget about our great mighty soldiers,
They sacrificed themselves for our safety and protection and our country.
We will never forget those who helped the army.
We will remember them in our hearts, the people who volunteered to join in the army.
Devoted their life for our benefit.
We will miss the army that died and went to heaven.
We will miss the men that were brave.
They fought for life and trust.
They lived and they felt dawn and they never gave up on their hopes and beliefs.
They were cold and hungry and they fought bravely for years striving for world peace.

Anton Alino (10)
Landau Forte Academy QEMS, Tamworth

Remember Me

R emember all the times we had fun but now because of war we can't.
E ven if we don't see each other remember me.
M emories we had, fun ones, miserable ones but we are still here.
E very day that passes by I think of you.
M any times I have missed you but you need to remember me.
B ecause I might never see you again because of the war.
E njoy your time as long as you can.
R emember me, don't forget me when you are at war.

M ake sure you stay safe and you are careful.
E mbrace the time we had together.

Nedelina Stefanova (11)
Landau Forte Academy QEMS, Tamworth

Invisible War Injuries

Safe on home turf,
Uniform put away,
Discharge papers signed,
Unfortunately, the war never ended that day.

She might have survived the tour,
But she cannot escape her own mind,
Flashbacks of the unimaginable,
Peace can be impossible to find.

Physical injuries are treatable,
Invisible ones not so much,
There's no cure for PTSD,
Not a bandage, prosthetic limb or a crutch.

Help and support is out there,
But we must open up more doors,
We need to keep our soldiers safe,
While they are fighting their own personal wars.

Ashton Bulmer (11)
Landau Forte Academy QEMS, Tamworth

Peace And War

War is harm
War is a big threat
War is scary
War is violent

Peace is what the world wants
Peace is kind
Be kind and you'll see
Let light in and be bright

War is fighting
War is trying to make you do, or give up something
War is hurtful to all involved
War is destructive
War is dangerous
War ruins lives

Peace is nature
Peace is soothing
Peace means no harm
Be kind and be caring, that's what peace is
Peace means no wars
Peace means love
Peace is what the world needs.

Katie Mason (11)
Landau Forte Academy QEMS, Tamworth

Evacuee - I'm All Alone Now

I'm all alone now - I have no name.
There are lots of children, we're all the same.
Just a number, hung around my neck.
Just one last look, I need to check.

Suitcase and gas mask in my hand.
There are some things I don't understand.
I will be safe, but I've been sent away,
I don't know where I'm going to stay.

The image of Mother gets smaller and smaller,
I'd do anything now just to hug her.
The steam train chugs down the track,
I have no idea when I'll be back.

Aimee Jarratt (12)
Landau Forte Academy QEMS, Tamworth

The Ones We Will Never Forget

Lest we forget, we pause in solemn grace,
To honour those who fought in the darkness of a place.
Through fields of strife and skies so grey,
They fought for our lives with a price to pay.

In the field of poppies, memories occupy.
With those who marched side by side, with hearts of gold, they took the lead.
Lest we forget their noble creed.

With gratitude we treasure their brave stand,
Their legacy lives on this land
We honour them, the brave in every place.

Terlea Tune (11)
Landau Forte Academy QEMS, Tamworth

Remember Them!

R est in peace the soldiers who sacrifice for us who live.
E ngland mourns the deaths of those who were killed.
M any poppies bloom in the damp soil of the trench field.
E vacuees sent home and not having a family to go to.
M ost buildings bombed in London killing thousands.
B lood hopelessly covering weapons and people.
E normous amounts of countries brought into battle.
R ivalries destroying nations and businesses!

Eliza Price (11)
Landau Forte Academy QEMS, Tamworth

Sadness Of War

War!

The return of dads and sons never coming back to see family again
The pain that some people couldn't fight
The emotional feelings of moms and children not being a full family again
Never having a walk
A breakfast, lunch, dinner
Never having a hug
Never having a conversation
Never being with them ever again
Not being able to have just a...
Smile

War!

George Stokes (12)
Landau Forte Academy QEMS, Tamworth

Lest We Forget

Lest we forget.
Lest we forget all the soldiers who died for us,
Sacrificing themselves for us,
Giving up their lives for us,
Doing what they could for us,
We must honour them,
We must remember them,
We must not forget them,
Fighting so we could live our lives,
To the end of their lives,
We must remember them,
And the sacrifices they made for us,
Lest we forget.

Isabelle Caile (15)
Landau Forte Academy QEMS, Tamworth

My Future Job, Aviation

High in the sunny sky,
My aircraft turns blue violet...

Flying along to Hong Kong,
Hours and hours back and forth like ping pong.
Eagles go past in the burning blue,
Sunset silence not even like woooh.

As it turns dark to night, the wings flash,
Nothing except dark as we go through the sky, dash.
Engines accelerate almost there to land,
The flight has been grand.

Tommy Rooke (11)
Landau Forte Academy QEMS, Tamworth

War And Peace

War is anger and war is sad
War is fighting and war is bad
War is dying and war is crying
War is shocking and war is frightening
War is a terrible thing
Peace is hope and peace is calm
Peace is family and peace is happy
Peace is loving each other and peace is kindness
Peace is a great thing
Which we can all find inside us.

Tristan Boyce (11)
Landau Forte Academy QEMS, Tamworth

War And Peace

W ar is damaging and destructive.
A rmed fighting causes devastation.
R avaged countries struggle to recover.

P eace is what we hope for.
E quality is what we want.
A nger has no place here.
C alm and peaceful life.
E ach and every one of us deserves peace and happiness.

Olivia Lawson (12)
Landau Forte Academy QEMS, Tamworth

Lest We Forget

Lest we forget those who found a new place,
Leaving their families to try and stay safe.
Never forgetting the ones they loved,
They were all truly beloved.

Lest we forget those who lost their life,
Trying so hard to hope they'll survive.
Never knowing if they'll have a family,
Hoping it will end happily.

Bethany Hunt (11)
Landau Forte Academy QEMS, Tamworth

How Important Soldiers Are To Me

Lest we forget
About the soldiers, our fighters
As without them
We would not be
They fought for our lives
And their souls should still survive
They gave their lives for ours
And emotions were their special power
The least we can do is remember
All of the members
Lest we forget.

Mia Plant (14)
Landau Forte Academy QEMS, Tamworth

Lest We Forget

Soldiers go to war
For the country they are fighting for
Friends and family are upset
They will really miss them - lest we forget

Soldiers in war are dying
Friends and family are crying
Bad news rocks them to the core
They aren't coming back - the sadness of war.

Samuel Martin (11)
Landau Forte Academy QEMS, Tamworth

Consequences Of War

War is sad
War is mad

War tears us apart
Peace brings us together

War is painful
Peace is healing

War is sad
War is mad

But peace is happiness in the eyes of me and you.

Samuel Rochfort (11)
Landau Forte Academy QEMS, Tamworth

Remember Them

In 1949,
Peace was declared
This brought happiness to the soldiers,
Who were no longer scared.
Every year I wear a little poppy,
As red as red can be,
To show that I remember,
Those who fought for me.

Mitchell Flounders (12)
Landau Forte Academy QEMS, Tamworth

Charging Into Battle

Charging into battle,
Not knowing what will come,
Never showing fear,
Marching at the pier,
Protecting the civilians,
Saving many billions,
While sadly losing millions.

Reece Evans (14)
Landau Forte Academy QEMS, Tamworth

War

War
Heroic, heart-wrenching
Praising, permitting, promoting
Combat, conflict, conquest, contention
Praying, promising, proliferating
Inhumane, inescapable
War.

Xenon Dunn (14)
Landau Forte Academy QEMS, Tamworth

Lest We Forget

The view of war and death
My heart sinking.
My family worrying where I am.
My sorrows leaving my soul.
My friends lying on their deathbeds.
I just want to go home to my family,
My friends, I wanted to grow old with them,
Partying, drinking.
But no, I'm here.
Wondering what I did to deserve this pain and horror.
I just want to die.
At home on my deathbed.
But no, I'm lying in a broken-down hospital.
With a few hours to live.
Not being able to see my kids for the last time.
My wife getting a letter to tell her of my demise.
For my final say Dear Diary,
I hope I see them again.
Whether it is in heaven or hell,
I hope I see them again.

Harriet Broughton-Read
Leeds East Academy, Seacroft

Soldiers

Grey skies
Sad eyes
Big boots

Happy eyes
Blue skies
Heavy helmets

We remember our soldiers with red poppies
We stand up tall
We are brave
We won't forget.

Alanna Collis (4)
Lings Primary School, Lings

Not Dead Yet

In the haunting silence where empty eyes reveal,
Mind-forged prisons echo with silence,
Left alone I fall apart, the world crumbles away,
Swallowed whole, am I dead?

Lost in a hurricane of pain and fear,
Not dead, but not living. It stands
Innocent lives shattered in seconds,
Two thuds, one bullet, one dead the other half a man,
A trigger's pull, some bloody hand, lives ripped apart.

"Get me out, get me out," they say it's in my head,
They can say what they like, these scars say it all,

Three seconds...
Three seconds...
Three seconds more...
Crash...
I lose control, red blood, flashing lights
Bashful thoughts, careless wants, blinded explosions
Crying, dying, a brutal reality we can't fight it,

"It's all in my head," the world's in disarray,
Dying, I'm dying, we're dying,

Sometimes I see ghosts, their ghosts
In passing hallways and staircases

Their limp bodies line the streets,
Their blood staining innocent hands,

Like a loaded gun we fire away, too young for this,
Praying the floor won't fall through again,
I'm losing my mind, the agony consuming me,

Silence driving me insane, emptiness, the dead,
Powering through struggles,
I didn't survive the war to given to this trouble,

Their screams echo through the corridors of my mind,
War and memories entwined.

If the war didn't kill, memories won't either,
Bullets, bombs pierce the air, I'm alive, but not quite living, half a man
Memories turn to ghosts, their spirits drag down
The unspoken fear, I'm past repair.

Broken bodies, broken souls, I've fallen to pieces,
Not dead yet, still breathing.

Phoebe Jakubas (13)
Loughborough Amherst School, Loughborough

War

They all marched off and saluted their master,
Fourteen months, they said.
It was bloodshed.

In November, we all must remember.
Bombs. People. Sadness on land.

On Christmas Day they played football.

Tanks blown into smithereens.
The gunshots last forever.

So, think of them and all they lived for,
And let us not forget.

Tobias Wiltshire
Louth Academy, Louth

Lest We Forget

Conflict as the late autumn approaches,
And children are driven away from their homes in trains.
They don't understand.
On the railway, no food, no money,
They wonder why, going away from their parents.
On a journey from London to Cornwall,
With the poppies, this place is safer.
They can't bear it.
Memories of their loved ones, they have innocence,
They wonder why the German soldiers do not.
Needing to be here, though all wish not,
Yet this place is calmer, nicer, quieter.
An evacuation place.
But the gunning must stop, before they return home,
They wonder why, will they be gone?
They will remember.

Charlie Sheldrick (9)
Marshgate Primary School, Richmond

Remembrance Day

R emember those who fought and are fighting,
E very choice they made a massive difference,
M aking us to be how we are now,
E very choice was the best choice.
M oments that you would never forget,
B ringing pride and success not only to them,
R aising pride to everyone.
A lthough they have passed away, their memory lives on,
N ovember is the month this day takes place,
C reating inspiration to many people in the world,
E leven will bring the moment of silence for...

Remembrance Day.

Aahil Upil
Marshgate Primary School, Richmond

The Poppies Grow

The poppies grow in rows and rows,
Filling up the battlefields.
Not a single tulip or rose,
The poppies, the only flower that grows.

You look, you would not know,
The screams and torture and the guns that would blow.
Now all that lies there are the fragile flowers,
To show us those who fought in the wars for powers.

So remember those who fought for us,
Remember those who gave their lives for us.
Think of them and the peace we have now,
How could we forget them, how, just how?

Lily Schofield (10)
Marshgate Primary School, Richmond

Peace

P eople should remember the people who lost their lives for us.
E veryone respect the soldiers who gave us freedom.
A ge doesn't matter, everyone take the two minutes to remember them.
C ould people at least take a day to remember the past.
E veryone remember them.

Remember them please.

Clara Anstey
Marshgate Primary School, Richmond

Remembrance

In World War One, which was long ago
Soldiers fought to protect us
After it had finished
Poppies started to grow

We remember those
And respected them
By bringing silence
Poppies started to grow

As are heads are hung low
We think and pray
For the people who lost their lives
Poppies started to grow.

Vienna-Pervin Upil (9)
Marshgate Primary School, Richmond

Silence

On the 11th day of the 11th month there is silence,
To honour the sacrifice of the fallen soldiers there is silence,
To bring hope to those fighting there is silence,
Because of this,
On the 11th day of the 11th month there is silence.

Ivor Richmond (9)
Marshgate Primary School, Richmond

War

Poppies grow
In Flanders fields
Across the land of conflict
Row on row people passed
The bullets, the deaths, it was everywhere
Under the trenches, over the trenches, it was terror
Remember your loved ones.

Cormac Lavery (10)
Marshgate Primary School, Richmond

Never Forget

Those we've lost, but never forgotten.
Those we've remembered, but never lost.
Never forget the ones we've loved, because they will always be in our hearts.
Look at the stars and remember.

Rohan Dinan (9)
Marshgate Primary School, Richmond

The Poppies Grow

After the horrific war,
after the screams,
after the loud gunshots,
the poppies grow,
giving such beauty to the battlegrounds,
as the poppies grow,
in Flanders fields.

Dogu Goktepe (9)
Marshgate Primary School, Richmond

Peace

Soldiers fighting for a better future,
Creating peace and hope for the next generations,
Think of those who lost their lives,
Trying to protect our country,
Remember them.

Molly Conneely (9)
Marshgate Primary School, Richmond

Peace

P eace is quiet, peace is calm.
E veryone is in harmony.
A ll together, friend not foe.
C ould world peace be real.
E veryone is in peace.

Isla Vannet
Marshgate Primary School, Richmond

Lest We Forget

The people were chosen to fight,
They all had a lot of fright,
The innocent children had to shoot the targets,
The dogs were made into communicators,
If they were no good they would kill the dogs,
Then the pigeons, they all had one foot,
Which was very sad,
They delivered messages,
Then the camels, people rode on them,
And the donkeys too,
People died in fear,
Of never seeing loved ones again,
They all hoped for peace,
They all received a bullet to the head,
The monstrous creature, who was Adolf Hitler,
Killed himself then people went home to see loved ones,
All the people and animals that died are looked up to,
Then there was beauty,
Poppies grew all over the wounds,
Now that is why we celebrate Remembrance Day.

Jenson Byrne (11)
Medina College, Newport

November 11th

Such amazing weather on November 11th,
Swaying breeze and clear skies above.
Memorials shining bright,
And people spreading love.

We remember the men and women that have passed,
And the animals that have fallen.
However the poppies are never forgotten,
With their sweet scent and pollen.

Red flowers with a deep meaning,
Filled with vast history.
Yet every year still remain,
Which still remains a mystery.

Even to this year we still celebrate,
In different ways we commemorate.
Holding a silence for a period of time,
And selling poppies at a rapid rate.

But every year on November 11th,
We celebrate the sacrifice of valiant soldiers.
How they risked their lives for us,
And we still honour them to this day.

Lucy Archer (13)
Medina College, Newport

A Legacy Of Love

Fallen soldiers,
We stand on your shoulders,
We carry your legacy,
We carry it with generosity.

Your bravery is unmatched,
Your courage is shown in a match,
The poppies are your souls,
Defeating all the trolls.

The red represents your blood,
Your love for the country is like a flood,
The green for the uniform you wore,
To put an end to this awful war.

The poppies have sprouted,
To show the horses you mounted,
60+ million 880,000 of which UK soldiers,
Had to overcome the lifeless boulders.

Today we will wear the poppy,
To represent your story,
The lives that were taken,
Shall never be forgotten.

Georgia Wilkins (11)
Medina College, Newport

My Remembrance Poem

We remember them, the brave and true
Who stood for us, and fought anew
In every battle, on every shore
They gave their lives, and so much more

We honour them with every year
With poppies red, and solemn tears
For those who fell, and those who bled
We bow our heads, and honour the dead

We remember them, the fallen few
And pledge to never forget what they do
For freedom, justice, and the right
They fought and died, for us tonight

So let us honour them, with every breath
For their sacrifice, we are forever blessed
On this Remembrance Day, we stand tall
And remember those who gave their all.

Leland Arnell (13)
Medina College, Newport

Poem Of Poppies

In Flanders' fields, the poppies blow
Between the crosses row and row
That marked our place; and in the sky
The larks still bravely singing, fly.

A sea of living crimson caught my eye
Beneath the pastel of an English sky
An oriental splendour, out of place
Where soft-toned pastures etch the tranquil face

In summertime, a silken poppied sea
Is like Mother Nature's generosity,
That shimmered in the early morning sun
Held out its cup of joy to everyone.

I will wear a little poppy
As red as can be
To show that I remember
Those who fought for me.

William Barbero (12)
Medina College, Newport

Lest We Forget

As the sacrificial battlegrounds were set,
the soldiers' end might soon be met,
They walked into battle,
confidence at the highest level.
After all, it will end soon,
it won't cause any harm they assume.

Little did they know it was the war of their time,
they thought it wouldn't cost them a dime.
It'll be fine, they said,
Half of them came back dead.

Their souls were halfway to death's door,
Couldn't life just give them some more?
It was good for no one,
Bad for everyone.

Jack Day (11)
Medina College, Newport

The Poppies

The poppies we wear are red,
representing those who are dead,
those who lost their lives,
who made the ultimate sacrifice.

War is not just a part of our past,
sadly peace will never last,
so take a moment to open your eyes,
as hope is often based on lies.

Through the dusty skies the bombs will drop,
so loud you will not hear the tick of a clock,
bringing terror, bloodshed and tears,
everyone will be consumed by their fears.

Bubbles Barton (11)
Medina College, Newport

War Poem

I can't forget that I lost my family to this
All I need is a moment of bliss
My heart just tore
To the sound of this horrifying war
I just need love
But my family have already flown to the sky like a dove
All I need is some peace
But I already know I'll soon be deceased
All this way I've been lured
I know I can't be cured.

Chloe Lewin (12)
Medina College, Newport

Lest We Forget

Lest we will never forget those who fell in these fields,
The sadness of war yet they still fought,
Courage of a lion in their solemn hearts,
The hope of peace spread across millions,
Still hurting people going to war,
Still missing those who have drunk their cup of sacrifice,
Heroes when they return.

Jessie Goring (11)
Medina College, Newport

Remembrance Day Poem

Poppies are red, their hearts were full
They gave their life so you didn't have to
They gave it their all so the least we could do is
Stand for two minutes and stand for them all.

Nicholas Waghorn (13)
Medina College, Newport

Peace In Your Violence

In the battlefield, chaos unfolds,
Where stories of bravery and sorrow are told.
Soldiers march, their hearts filled with might,
Fighting for freedom, in the day and the night.
Explosions echo, shaking the ground,
As war's relentless symphony resounds.
Tears of anguish, cries of despair,
War's heavy burden, it's hard to bear.
But within the darkness, a glimmer of light,
Hope emerges, shining so bright.
For in the hearts of those who fight,
A longing for peace, burning so bright.
Let us strive for harmony and unity,
To end the cycle of this brutality.
May compassion and understanding prevail,
And war's destructive power finally fails...

Bryony Roberts
Nicholas Chamberlaine School, Bedworth

In A War

The stench of sweat and mud
It fills my lungs.
I can hardly breathe
With what strength I have left
I look around myself wearily.
I look at the lives lost.
And then at the battlefield
Death. Death is all I can see.
The realisation that this war makes no sense.
Why oh why did this war start?
In the trenches
Sick, dying soldiers are forced to fight.
Not just on the German side
But the British soldiers are losing hope.
Until this dreadful war is over
We promise we will fight.
Through the sadness of a loss
Or the terror of the battle
Or the news of a loved one fading away.
"Whether it was a bomb or an attack."
Or so the history teachers say.
We fought with depression and anger.
But we never gave up on Britain.
Now I'm speaking in past tense.
As I too have faded away

Lest We Forget - Beyond The Battlefield

But I have not lost all.
My body as do many others.
Lies underground now.
But you never as once a year you celebrate Remembrance Day
For the ones that were lost
And for the survivors that live the trauma
The two-minute silence
May not seem like much.
But all us ghosts
Appreciate the effort.
For all the soldiers who fought in either war
Deserved to be remembered.
Remembered like a family member.
Even though a stranger
All soldiers who fought bravely
They were all so amazing.
It was a sad lonely time.
For those who struggle and grieve
Many were lost.
And somehow more than a hundred years later
I still have that stench in my lungs.
The memories of the bodies
Of my friends from down at the pub
Who now lie beneath your feet?
And the ones alive to them I say.
"You survived a war; you are a true hero."

Brooke Till
Northview House School, Kilbarchan

Shall We Ever Forget?

Shall we ever forget,
About them marching about,
Fighting in war so they could come
Home to their families, with smiles on their faces?

Shall we ever forget,
When they suffered in silence with
Trauma and illnesses,
Living in trenches as they're getting
Diseases and serious illnesses with their trauma.

Shall we ever forget,
When their families got letters
Home to their loved ones, that they
Were bold and brave enough to fight,
But didn't make it home.

Shall we ever forget,
Their peace and silence, as they didn't come home.

Shall we ever forget,
Our sweet souls,
Who risked their lives for our country,
They gave all they could give.
Their going down of the sun,

We will remember them.

Summer Morris (14)
Norton Canes High School, Cannock

Lest We Forget

This war has affected so many lives
Nobody knows how it leaves the wives
Let's hope everyone remembers
To pay their respects in November!

Thank goodness for the armed forces
Years ago, the war even claimed our horses
This war has torn many families
Life after war is hard in the valleys

We feel pride
For the soldiers that died
The soldiers were brave
In their trench cave.

Lacey-Mae Owens
Norton Canes High School, Cannock

Poppies

To all the soldiers who died day by day
Not lilies, not roses but poppies we lay
They grew in the battlefields, row upon row
Covering the horrors of the conflict long ago
Growing there innocently, petals sore
Reminding us all of the dead and the war
A symbol of hope, they stand so proud
Covering the soil just like a shroud
So wear your poppy with pride and joy
Memories of their sacrifice we must not destroy
The poppy, a symbol of hope and peace
Praying that all the war and conflict will cease.

Apryl Jennings (12)
Oldbury Wells School, Oldbury Wells

Remembering The Forgotten

All I remember is the sound we fear
Gunshots ringing in my ear
My friends and colleagues crawling over bloodstained land
All because we were afraid to stand
One shot, one dead
We risked our lives so people could be fed
I really wish you could have survived
Just to see how we have thrived
It was too bad your parents made you volunteer
You could have been an engineer
So remember, remember this day in November
The day the poppies grew.

Ben Morris Baker (11)
Oldbury Wells School, Oldbury Wells

Look For The Light

When I was young,
And the darkness hung,
I feared the monsters that crawled along the wall,
They had slimy scales, daggers as teeth and figures so tall.
I would look for the landing light flickering through the crack,
And my nightmares would melt away and never come back.

So, I always remember to look for the light,
Not only in the night.

When I was older,
Darkness got bolder,
And it started to attack the land.
So, when it got late lights were banned.
gunfire, screams and explosions could be heard,
but I had my tea light close and it wouldn't be stirred.
so, I always remember to look for the light,
so, I know I can still fight.

Not long after,
When darkness got dafter,
I heard it storm through the front door,
So, my family and I hid beneath the floor.
They screamed like devils, destroyed my house, and horribly swore,
But I had my family, my light, so I knew I was safe and I cared no more.

So, I always remember to look for the light,
So, I know my heart is still beating and bright.

Later that week,
When darkness was at its peak,
I heard it smash bullets and bricks through the glass.
I was in the saferoom first so I waited for my family to pass.
10 minutes, 10 hours, 10 days,
I was alone in the darkness without a ray,
So now I do not have any light,
And it's my turn to say goodnight.

All I have to say,
Is war is not okay.

Jenny Queally (12)
Parklands Academy, Chorley

A Conversation In 1914

We all huddled in the living room,
A gust of silence weeps through the already-cracked window,
Father clears his throat,
His eyes widened,
There was sweat dripping off his forehead,
Little did we know that he just received the letter that changed his life.
He shed a slight tear.
I asked him, "What's wrong Papa?"
He hesitated for a moment, then took a deep breath,
"I am going to war," he blurted
Mother dropped the book she was reading,
Head in her hands,
"I am leaving tomorrow morning,"
Sorrow filled the confined space,
I ran up to him and sobbed in his arms,
Wishing that tomorrow wouldn't exist,
Wishing that the sun wouldn't rise,
Wishing that the moment would last forever.
It's been a year since that happened,
We got a letter from France last week,
Father was killed in battle.
How I wished that moment wouldn't end,
Of us in the freezing living room,

Our last moment together.
Mother isn't coping.
She doesn't smile as often as she used to.
There is a war going on, there is nothing to be happy about.
It went cold, all over again.
I can barely remember him,
His smile, his face,
All just another faded memory,
Life is still different without him,
But we have worse to worry about.
Lest we forget.

Izzy Frohock (12)
Parklands Academy, Chorley

Faceless

They're home.
At last safe and sound.
That was the goal, for them to be homebound.
You hear news of their return.
Yet no screams of joy, only screams of hearts that burn.
No man came back the same.
The sporadic rate of knocks at doors,
To tell those wives they no longer had to endure
The wait for hope; they were widowed at last.
No man came back the same.
Whilst governors danced away their false culpability,
Barmaids sing to now-silenced pubs,
To those who only leave empty glasses and faith behind.
No man came back the same.
They once laughed you know,
But kicking clay in death traps, they called tunnels, does not allow a moment of mercy in one's own mind.
What is laughter? But a fake cry.
No man came back the same.
"Damn them for what they did to you," she says.
Silence sits, as those words leave a prolonged echo between them.
No man came back the same.
As he walks down the street, on his own,
The surrounding world torments him to remember the memories that once were.

He looks at his reflection, but sees no one looking back. Nothing was the same.

Safiya Zentani (15)
Parklands Academy, Chorley

What Do You Know About War?

What do you know about war?
About a terrified child.
About his doll that fell from his hand.
About a family who fled leaving their hot morning tea on the table.
About a bored house missing the laughter of children.

War takes place between people who don't know each other.
If people took the time to get to know each other, they probably wouldn't want to kill each other.

War takes away children's rights and their simple dreams.
No one can feel the pain, only the people who experience it.
And no one can feel how people in war feel.

People wish to live with their family forever but some dreams don't come true.
What people in war know about is death.
You can die any second.

What general people know about war is not what the people who experience it feel like.
They feel scared more than you think.
Give children their childhood.

Hind Fares (13)
Parklands Academy, Chorley

I Was Once A Child

I was once a child, born in ruins, in fire, in death
I was born in Gaza, where we awaited our final breath
The drones, they came to bomb us, and my parents didn't survive
They had to pull me from the rubble, a child but barely alive.

Growing up in Gaza, all the children learned,
The sky kills, the houses hurt and the fire that ensues burns
There was nobody to heal you, nobody to help
Nobody to tuck you in when a nightmare made you yelp.

Growing up in this world of sadness, of pain and of grief
Makes you treasure the moments of happiness, though they are very brief Please help us in our struggle, in our strife and in our pain,
Blood and bodies fill our country and our hands are bound in chains.

Róisín Cunningham
Parklands Academy, Chorley

Happy To Be Here

Happy to be here
As tears blind my eye
There's nothing I can do
But sit here and cry

Happy to be here
That's all I can muster
As I clutch the cold hands
Of what's left of my mother

Happy to be here
I can solely exist
I'm only missing an eye
What's left is a gift

Happy to be here
My ears start to ring
Explosions and massacres
I feel nothing.

Raghad Elhabal (14)
Parklands Academy, Chorley

A Narrative Woven From The Fabric Of The Fight

The pen becomes a sword, the paper a shield,
In verse, the scars find a voice to wield.
Through metaphors, a shallow escape,
Like fastening wounds with sticky tape.

So, let the ink bleed on the page,
A therapy born from the war's rage.
My wounded heart, a battleground,
Where healing is a distant, elusive sound.
A narrative woven from the fabric of the fight.

Lincoln Stothers (15)
Parklands Academy, Chorley

Lest We Forget

Though we are dead, our love still lives on in the people and places we remember.
A poppy of peace lies on loved ones as they revisit our shared stories,
but they know they will see us again.
Death is hard to get over but easy to happen,
peace will forever live on.
It's hard to find love at first, but once found, you can never get over.
Our battlefield cries can be heard from miles away
as can the gunshots as we say our farewell.
As the poppy reappears, so do the tears,
but everyone will fly upwards one day.
Our graves are decorated with the red flowers
each one placed by the earth's heart.
Being dead doesn't mean we don't have a heart,
but our hearts will always be British as will the fields we fought on.
As each gunfire is fired through our captains' hearts,
we pass the bright torch down through generations to hold up high, forever.
Life is everything, so do make the most of it, like we all did,
no matter how old we were when we died, 18, 32, 50 or 20,
we all lived to the best of our ability and for the best reason - peace.
Revenge is never the right option, neither is war

so, when you look down at your poppy, which you're proudly
wear during the small silence, remember us, remember
Britain - your past, your future, you.
Remember the songs we used to sing,
the stories we used to tell us!
Never let us go,
like we never let go of our determination.
Our spirit will lift you up like wings, soaring through the sky.
Our love will caress your heart, through highs and lows.
Our memories will bring you inner peace as will the thought
of seeing us again.
Your hope.
Your love.
Your determination.
It all reminds you of us.
Horrible things happen but remember the positives,
our memories
As we fly to our forever home in the sky.

India Akass (11)
Portsmouth High School, Southsea

Hope

Hope dies at the end.
Where conflicts from a man,
Spread to a much bigger span.
Hope dies. Hope dies at the end.
Where children await.
For what is now the army's bait.
Hope dies. Hope dies at the end.
Our own countless tragedies.
Are just their abnormalities.
Hope dies. Hope dies at the end.
But when we are done.
And all is now won.
Hope dies. Hope dies at the end.
So now I look across a sea of blood.
It comes down. Down as a flood.
Hope dies. Hope dies at the end.
Though, when all hearts rise.
And all but bloodstained lies.
Hope begins anew. And peace is out to lend.

Mia Rosenberg (14)
Queenswood School, Hatfield

The Letter

We waited anxiously by the door.
Breath baited, hearts hitched in our tiny throats.
A single, white envelope dropped through the door.
The world went quiet, no one dared to move.
My mother pushed everyone aside,
Busily sweeping up the cream-coloured, crinkled letter, with a blood-red stamp slapped on top.
As if the finery and fanciness would be able to make up for the contents.
We heard our mother's scream, but no one rushed to comfort her.
No one was able to move.
The breath escaped our lungs by our barely beating hearts,
As we fell on top of one another in a flood of fear and pain.

Issy Naylor (15)
Queenswood School, Hatfield

Young Writers Information

We hope you have enjoyed reading this book – and that you will continue to in the coming years.

If you're the parent or family member of an enthusiastic poet or story writer, do visit our website **www.youngwriters.co.uk/subscribe** and sign up to receive news, competitions, writing challenges and tips, activities and much, much more! There's lots to keep budding writers motivated!

If you would like to order further copies of this book, or any of our other titles, then please give us a call or order via your online account.

Young Writers
Remus House
Coltsfoot Drive
Peterborough
PE2 9BF
(01733) 890066
info@youngwriters.co.uk

Join in the conversation!
Tips, news, giveaways and much more!

YoungWritersUK YoungWritersCW
youngwriterscw youngwriterscw